Why Jesus Came

Why Jesus Came

By BEVERLY SCHULTZ MULLINS
and BONNY VAUGHT

Illustrated by Isa Barnett
Gustav K. Wiencke, Editor

LUTHERAN CHURCH PRESS / PHILADELPHIA

LCA SUNDAY CHURCH SCHOOL SERIES

This pupil's Reader is accompanied by a Teacher's Guide, *We Want to Know,* and an Activity Packet. This material has been prepared for use in Term 1 in the Sunday church school (1-1). The general theme for the year is "We Want to Know."

Contents

We Want To Know

Once, long ago, in a land far away, there lived a man who was strong and good. He was loving and kind. And God was with him. His name was Jesus.

Wherever Jesus went, people felt close to God. He showed them how much God loved them. He helped them to know and love God.

That was long ago, but Jesus still loves and helps you. Because you know Jesus, you know that God loves you. Because Jesus came, you can feel close to God.

This is a book for "We want to know" questions about the wonderful story of Jesus in the Bible. In Sunday church school you may think and talk about the stories in this book. At home you can read this book with Father or Mother. What can you tell Father and Mother about the pictures? Which story do you like best? Can you tell them something about *why Jesus came?*

PART
1

When God
Sent Jesus

GOD . . . loved us and sent his Son.

1 JOHN 4:10

The Very Special Promise

Nazareth was a little town in Galilee. It was built half-way up a hill and the small square houses were made of grey stones or yellow bricks of dried mud. Around the town were fields and orchards.

Far away a busy highway passed through the valley. Camels from faraway lands carried rich treasure along the road, but they never carried it to Nazareth. Kings traveled along this road, but they never came to Nazareth. Nazareth was not an important town and no big road went up to it.

The people who lived in Nazareth were farmers who plowed the land. They were shepherds who took care of their sheep in the hills. They were carpenters who made strong tables and benches. They were mothers who rocked their babies to sleep in the little white houses.

But one day, something very important did happen in Nazareth. It happened to a young woman named Mary. From the doorway of her house Mary could see nearly the whole town. She could see the street where the shoemakers lived. She could see the street of the men who wove cloth. And she could see the busy street of the carpenters.

"Soon I will live in the street of the carpenters," Mary said to herself. She was going to marry Joseph, the carpenter, and then she would go to live in his house.

Mary liked to think about Joseph. She liked the way his dark eyes smiled at her. She liked his kind ways. Joseph was not a rich man, but he was a good man. He loved God and he worked hard.

Maybe Mary was thinking about Joseph when the important thing happened. All at once the air seemed filled with light, even brighter than the sun. And there, in front of Mary, stood an angel of God!

"God is with you, Mary!" the angel said.

Mary felt afraid. She did not know what to say.

"Do not be afraid, Mary," the angel said. "God is going to send his son to live in the world. And he has chosen you to be the baby's mother. You must call the baby Jesus, because he will bring God's love to all people. He will be more important than any baby who was ever born, for he will show everyone what God is really like."

"But how can I be his mother?" Mary said. "I am not married yet."

"Just believe God," the angel told her. "God can make it happen."

"I do believe God," Mary said. "I will do whatever God wants."

For many days Mary thought about the angel. She sang a song of joy for the wonderful thing that was going to happen.

"My heart is glad, for God is good.

I give thanks to God with my whole heart!"

An angel told Joseph what would happen, too. "God wants you to take care of Mary and the baby Jesus," the angel said. "He wants you to love the baby and teach him."

So Mary and Joseph were married, and Mary went to live at Joseph's house in the street of the carpenters. And they got ready to welcome the new baby, the little Son of God.

Happy Birthday!

Everything was ready for the baby Jesus. Mary wove a soft, warm cradle of wool and hung it from the roof beams. Joseph carved a little goat out of wood for the baby to play with. Soon it would be time for the baby to be born.

Then one day a messenger rode up the hill to Nazareth. "The king wants to find out how many people live in his land," the messenger said. "Everyone must go to the place his family came from to have his name written down for the king."

And so Mary and Joseph had to leave their warm little house. They had to travel a long way to a town called Bethlehem. That was where Joseph's father and his grandfather had been born.

It was winter. Cold winds blew through the olive trees. Joseph did not like to take Mary on such a long, hard trip before the baby came.

"I am not afraid," Mary said. "God will take care of us."

For five days the donkey carried Mary on his back, while Joseph walked along beside them. Up over the hills they climbed. Down into the valleys they went, and up into the hills again. With each step the donkey rocked gently from side to side. Mary thought about the baby son God was sending into the world. She made up a lullaby to sing to the baby:

Welcome, little Son of God,
Welcome, little Jesus!

It was night when Mary and Joseph came to Bethlehem. The air was frosty and the night sky was bright with shining stars. One star shone brighter than all the rest. "I have never seen a star so bright," Mary thought.

Mary felt tired now, and cold. She knew that very soon the baby would be born.

"There is a place in Bethlehem where tired travelers can stay," Joseph said. "Soon you will be warm and safe."

Joseph climbed the stairs to the inn. "My wife and I need a room," he told the man who took care of the inn. "We have come a long way, and we are tired and cold."

The man was sorry. "There is not one room left," he told Joseph. "Many travelers are in Bethlehem to-night. The inn is full of tired people."

"Do you know a place where we can go?" Joseph asked. "My wife is going to have a baby. She needs a place that is quiet and warm for the baby to be born."

The man thought. Then he said to Joseph, "Come with me."

Joseph followed him down the hill. He showed him a cave in the stony side of the hill. "This is where we keep the animals," the man said. "It is not as nice as a

room, but it is warm and dry. You are welcome to stay here."

There, in the quiet cave where an ox and a donkey had their home, the baby Jesus was born. Mary washed him and wrapped him in clean white cloths. She made a soft bed for him in a manger and laid him in the sweet-smelling hay.

"Sleep well," she said softly. "Sleep well, my little Jesus."

It was very early in the morning. The town of Bethlehem was sound asleep. Nobody there knew yet what God had done that night.

Mary and Joseph smiled as they watched the little Jesus, asleep in his manger bed. Mary sang softly,

Welcome, little Son of God,
Welcome, little Jesus!

When Jesus Was
Just As Old As You

When Jesus was just as old as you, he liked to watch Joseph, his father, in the carpenter shop. He liked to watch Joseph saw the wood and plane it smooth. He liked to watch him bore a hole with the drill. As he pulled the bow to one side, the drill turned so fast it seemed to sing. As he pushed it the other way, it sang again. The boy Jesus held the board to help Joseph.

Sometimes Joseph showed the boy Jesus how to pick out the best piece of wood to make a table leg. He showed him how to use the saw and he let him sweep the

shavings into a big pile. That was fun to do. Joseph was teaching Jesus to be a good carpenter.

When Jesus was just as old as you, he could reach up and touch the little box that hung on the doorpost of his house. Inside the box was a small piece of paper. It said, *You shall love the* LORD *your God with all your heart, and with all your soul, and with all your might.*

Even before Jesus was tall enough to reach the box himself, Joseph had lifted him up so that he could touch it. He had taught Jesus to say the words by heart.

"You must remember these words," Joseph told Jesus. "They remind us that God is more important than anything or anyone. God loves us and takes care of us. We must always love God best of all."

Every time Jesus went into the house or came out again, he touched the little box. He said the words over to himself,

> *You shall love the* LORD *your God with all your heart, and with all your soul, and with all your might.*

When Jesus was just as old as you, he liked to help his mother get water from the well. Jesus' little brother went along, too. Jesus held his hand so that he would not run away or get hurt.

All the mothers of Nazareth came to the well. On their heads they carried heavy jars full of water. Jesus

liked to see the bucket come up out of the well when his
mother pulled the rope. It made him think of a Bible
verse his mother liked to say:

> *Ho, every one who thirsts, come to the waters!*

"God gives the water," Jesus thought. "Thank you,
God, for the good water!"

When Jesus was just as old as you, he liked to go to school. Only boys went to Jesus' school. They sat on mats on the floor. At school Jesus was learning to write. He wrote with a lump of chalk on the stone floor or with a stick in smooth earth. He was learning to read, too. He wished he could read all the words in the big scrolls that told about God.

Jesus called his teacher "Rabbi." That means, "my teacher." The rabbi told the boys all about their country.

"We belong to God," he said. "God chose us to love and serve him."

The rabbi taught them the rules that would help them live as God's people. He told them about a great promise God had made long ago. "Some day God will send someone very special to help us," the rabbi said. "He will bring us God's love."

Jesus liked to wonder about that person God would send to bring his love to the world.

PART
2

Jesus and
the Children

JESUS said, "Let the children come to me."

MARK 10:14

God Loves You!
God Wants You!

When Jesus grew up, he went from town to town to tell people what God is like. One day Jesus came to a small town. How excited the people were! They ran from house to house to tell the news.

"Jesus has come to our town! Hurry! Come and see Jesus!"

Mothers hurried to finish their sweeping and baking. Fathers put away their work and closed their shops. Children ran home to ask if they could go, too. Everyone got ready to see Jesus.

A little boy named Joram clapped his hands. He was going to see Jesus, too. He skipped along between his father and mother.

When they came to the edge of the town, they saw Jesus talking to a large crowd of people.

"God loves you," Jesus told the people. "God is with you. He wants you to be in his family."

Joram listened to Jesus. He heard Jesus say that everyone must love God best of all. He heard Jesus tell the people that they must love one another, just as God loved them.

Joram's father lifted him up so he could see better. Joram could see Jesus' kind face and friendly smile. "I like him," Joram thought. "I wish I could talk to him."

"Can I?" he asked his father. "Can I talk to Jesus, too?"

"We will wait and see," his father said.

Joram waited and waited. Jesus talked to many people. He answered their questions. He explained many things that they wanted to know. All day long Jesus taught the people.

Joram was getting tired. First he hopped on one foot. Then he hopped on the other foot. He watched his shadow getting longer and longer as the sun sank lower in the sky.

"When can I talk to him?" Joram asked his father. "When can I talk to Jesus?"

"I don't know, Joram," his father said. "It is getting late and there are still many people who want to see Jesus. Some of them are sad. Some of them are lonely. Some of them are worried. They need God's help. They need to hear what Jesus tells them about God. They need to know what God wants them to do."

Joram looked at all the people waiting to see Jesus. "I know," he said. "But I wish I could talk to him, too. I think he likes children, too, Father."

"Of course he does, my son!" Joram's father gave him a hug. "But Jesus is tired, too, Joram. He has been talking to people since early this morning. See all the other boys and girls who are waiting? If Jesus talked to everybody, he would never be able to sleep."

Joram looked at the ground. He didn't want to cry, but it was hard to hold back the tears.

"I just wanted to talk to him for a minute," he said.
"Just for a minute."

Joram's father knew how much Joram wanted to
see Jesus.

"We will wait and see," he said.

The sun sank lower in the sky. Joram's shadow got
longer and longer. Some helpers of Jesus came toward
the place where the mothers and fathers were waiting
with their children. "You must go home now," they said.

"Jesus is tired. You must not bother him any more today."

"But the children want to see Jesus," the mothers and fathers said. "Couldn't they see him just for a minute?"

The men scolded the mothers and fathers. "It is too late," they said. "Take the children away."

Just then a strong voice said, "Let the children come to me!" It was Jesus!

"Do not stop them," Jesus said to his friends. "God loves them. God wants them in his family, too."

Jesus looked straight at Joram and smiled at him! Joram let go of his father's hand and ran right up to Jesus. "I'm Joram," he said. "You're not too tired to talk to us, are you?"

Jesus took Joram's hand. "No, Joram," he said. "I am never too tired to talk to you."

Joram sat down close to Jesus. Other children came running to see Jesus, too. Jesus said hello to all the boys and girls. He called each one by name. Then Jesus put his hand on the children's heads. "God loves you," he told them. "God wants you."

It was almost dark when Joram walked home between his father and mother. He felt warm and happy. "Jesus talked to me," he said. "Jesus talked to all of us."

The Boy Who Was Sick

What was happening on the road? Jesus heard loud voices. He saw a crowd of excited people. Some men were arguing with his helpers, the disciples.

Jesus walked toward the men. When they saw him coming, they hurried to meet Jesus.

"What are you talking about?" Jesus asked them. "What is the matter?"

Then one man said, "Teacher, I brought my son to see you. He is very sick. Sometimes he falls down in the street. His whole body gets stiff. He moans and tries to talk, but he cannot say any words. I asked your disciples to make him well, but they were not able to do it."

Jesus looked at his disciples. "That is what we were talking about," they explained. "These men were making fun of us because we could not heal the boy."

Jesus shook his head sadly.

"Bring your son to me," he said to the boy's father.

The father ran to get his son. He brought him to Jesus. Just then the sickness came to the boy again. He fell down on the ground and rolled around. Everyone could see how much the sickness hurt him.

Jesus felt sorry for the boy and his father. "How long has he had this sickness?" Jesus asked.

"Since he was a little boy," the father said. "Once he fell into the fire and nearly burned to death. Another time he fell into the water and nearly drowned. If you can do anything, please help us."

"*If* I can do anything!" Jesus said. "Why do you say *if* I can do anything? I can help anyone who really trusts me."

Then the father stretched out his hands to Jesus. "I do trust you," he cried. "Oh, please—help me to trust you even more."

Jesus bent down and spoke to the sickness in the boy. "Come out of him," he said. "Come out and never come back again."

The boy stopped rolling around. He lay very still.

The men looked at one another. "He is dead!" they said.

But Jesus took the boy's hand and helped him to get up. The boy stood up straight and tall. He smiled at Jesus. He was well! How glad the father was then! He thanked Jesus over and over again.

When the people had gone home, the disciples said to Jesus, "Why couldn't we make him well?"

"You did not ask God to help you," Jesus told them. "You did not trust God."

PART

3

How Jesus
Helped

He went about doing good and healing all . . . for
God was with him.

ACTS 10:38

When Jesus Came to Jericho

Outside the big city of Jericho a poor man sat by the side of the road. His name was Bartimaeus and he sat here every day. He hoped someone would give him a few coins so that he could buy bread.

Bartimaeus listened carefully to every sound because he could not see. He heard the quick tramp-tramp of the soldiers' feet. He heard the children laughing and

shouting. He heard the fathers and mothers talking about
things that were happening in their city.

Sometimes as he sat by the side of the road Bartimaeus heard people talking about a great teacher named
Jesus.

"He has done wonderful things," people said. "He
goes about everywhere, doing good and healing the sick."

"My friend's little boy was very sick with a high
fever," a soldier said. "Jesus made him well again."

"I know a man who was so sick he could not move,"
another man said. "His friends carried him to Jesus.
Now he walks around as well as I do!"

50

"He even makes deaf people able to hear!" said someone else.

"How can he do all these things?" someone asked.

"He says that God is with him."

Bartimaeus listened to the people talking. "If only I could get near Jesus," he thought. "Maybe he would help me, too."

One day Bartimaeus heard excited voices. He heard many people coming down the road. He heard shouting and cheering.

"What is it?" Bartimaeus asked. "What is happening?"

"It is Jesus from Nazareth," someone said. "Jesus is coming!"

Jesus from Nazareth! Bartimaeus was very excited. He heard the shouts and cheers coming closer and closer.

"Jesus!" he called out. "Lord Jesus, have mercy on me! Help me!"

The men near Bartimaeus were angry. "Be quiet!" they told him. "Do you think Jesus is interested in a blind beggar like you?"

But Bartimaeus did not listen to the men. He cried out even louder, "Jesus, have mercy on me! Help me!"

Jesus heard the cry for help. He looked around to see who it was. "Bring that blind man to me," he said.

Hands reached out to help Bartimaeus. As fast as he could, he hurried to Jesus.

"What do you want me to do for you?" Jesus asked.

Bartimaeus was so excited he could feel his heart pounding. "Teacher," he said, "please let me see."

Jesus put his hand on Bartimaeus' shoulder. "Because you trust me, you are well," he said.

It was true! One minute Bartimaeus could see nothing at all. Now he saw the kind face of Jesus. He saw the surprised people crowding around him. He saw the sun shining down on the city of Jericho.

Jesus moved on down the road. And Bartimaeus followed him, singing praise to God. And all the people shouted and cheered and thanked God for sending Jesus to love and help them.

The Man in the Tree

In the city of Jericho lived a very rich man named Zacchaeus. Zacchaeus had an important job, but he did not have many friends.

"Zacchaeus is not a good man," people said. "He does not love his country."

"He does not care about us at all," they said. "He only wants to make money for himself. Sometimes he even charges us more than is right."

Poor Zacchaeus. He was very lonely.

One day Zacchaeus heard the people shouting and cheering. He saw them running down the street, as if they were going to a big parade. He saw them standing all along the sides of the road.

"Someone very important must be coming," Zacchaeus thought. "I wonder who it is."

He tried to see over the heads of the people, but he was too short.

Then he heard someone shout, "Here he comes! Here comes Jesus!"

"Jesus is coming!" Zacchaeus thought. "I have heard of wonderful things Jesus does. I would like to see him, too."

He tried to push his way to the front of the crowd, but nobody would let him through.

He stood on tiptoe, but all he could see was the neck of the man in front of him.

Then Zacchaeus had an idea. Along the side of the road were some low trees. Their branches stretched right

out over the street. "If I could climb up there," Zacchaeus thought, "then I could see Jesus!"

So Zacchaeus ran down the street until he found a tree that was just right. Quickly he climbed up and slid out along one of the wide branches. It was a good spot. He could see the people running down the road, shouting and singing praises to God.

He noticed one man dancing and singing with joy. "Why, isn't that the blind beggar who always sits outside the city?" thought Zacchaeus. "But he isn't blind anymore!"

The crowd came closer. Now Zacchaeus could see Jesus!

And Jesus saw Zacchaeus, too. He stopped, right underneath the leafy branch where Zacchaeus was sitting.

"Zacchaeus," Jesus said, "come down right away. Today I am coming to your house to visit you!"

Zacchaeus was surprised. He scrambled down and hurried home with Jesus. He ordered his servants to get a fine dinner ready for Jesus. How proud and happy he was that Jesus wanted to visit him!

The people who saw what happened were surprised, too, but they were not happy. "Doesn't Jesus know what a bad man Zacchaeus really is?" they asked each other.

Jesus knew that Zacchaeus had done wrong things. But he also knew that Zacchaeus needed help. He needed a friend. Jesus loved Zacchaeus. Then another surprising thing happened. Zacchaeus looked up and told Jesus what he would do.

"From now on, I am going to live the way you want me to live," he promised. "Look, I am going to give half my money to poor people. And if I have cheated anybody, I will give him back all the money I took, and much more besides!"

Jesus was happy because Zacchaeus loved him and was going to try to be the kind of man God wanted him to be.

"God loves you, Zacchaeus," he said. "God is with you."

The Storm

It was a dark night. Thick clouds hid the moon. No stars were shining. On the lake of Galilee a little boat moved away over the quiet water. Jesus and his disciples were sailing across the big lake.

Suddenly a strong wind slapped heavy waves against the sides of the little boat. The disciples of Jesus pulled harder on the oars.

"A storm is coming," they said to one another. "We must get to shore as fast as we can!"

In the back of the boat, Jesus was asleep. All day long he had talked to people and healed their sicknesses. He was tired and needed to rest.

A strong, cold wind blew against the little boat and whipped the water into giant waves.

"Row harder!" the men shouted to one another. "If we don't get to shore soon, the waves will break our boat to pieces!"

They rowed as hard as they could. But they could
not get the boat to shore.

The wind blew stronger and stronger. The little
boat tossed like a toy on the rough, deep water.

The waves pounded against the sides of the wooden
boat. The old boat creaked and groaned and shivered as
the wind and waves smashed against it.

"Look!" shouted one of the disciples. "Water is coming into our boat!"

The waves were so high that the water crashed over the sides of the boat. The boat was filling with water!

Now the disciples were really afraid. They looked at the water filling the boat. "What can we do?" they cried. "We shall drown!"

Then someone thought of Jesus, still asleep in the stern of the boat. The disciples shook him to wake him up.

"Teacher, don't you see what is happening?" they cried. "Don't you care if we die?"

"Why are you afraid?" Jesus said to his friends. "I am with you. Don't you believe that I will take care of you?"

Then he spoke to the wind and the waves, "Peace! Be still!"

The wind stopped. The lake was very quiet again. The little boat rocked gently on the still water.

The friends of Jesus looked at one another. How could such a thing be? Only God was as powerful as that!

"Who is this man," they wondered, "that even the wind and sea obey him?"

More Than Enough

Every day great crowds of people came to see Jesus. So many people to tell about God's love! So many people who needed help! Sometimes Jesus and his friends did not even have time to eat.

One morning Jesus said to his twelve disciples, "You have worked hard. Come, let us find a quiet place and rest awhile."

So Jesus and his friends got into their boat. But some people who knew Jesus saw him. "He is going to sail to the other side of the lake!" they said.

As fast as they could, they ran around the lake and got to the other side before Jesus. On the way they told everyone they met, "Jesus is coming! Hurry! Come and see Jesus!"

From all the towns around the lake, people came running. Fathers and mothers. Boys and girls. Old people and young people. Sad people and sick people and lonely people. They did not stop to finish their work. They did not even stop to pack a lunch. They just ran to see Jesus!

When Jesus and his friends got out of their boat on the other side of the lake, they saw many people waiting for them. "These people need me," he thought. "They need to know that God is with them. They need to see that God can help them."

So Jesus led the way to a grassy place in the hills where everybody could see and hear him. And he began to teach the people. What a sight that was! Thousands and thousands of people, sitting on the green hillside, listening to Jesus.

Noontime came, and afternoon. And still the people stayed to listen. They did not notice how hungry they were.

When it was suppertime, the disciples came to Jesus. "It is getting late," they said. "The people must be very hungry. Send them away, so they can get something to eat."

But Jesus said, "You must give them something to eat now. They have a long way to walk. We cannot let them go home without food."

The disciples looked at one another. What could Jesus be thinking about? How could they feed so many people?

"Do you want us to go and buy food for all these people?" they asked. "You know we do not have so much money!"

"How much food do you have?" Jesus asked. "Go and see."

So the disciples went and counted the loaves of bread and the fish.

Then they said, "There are five little loaves of barley bread and two fish. That is all we have."

"It is enough," said Jesus.

Then Jesus told the people to sit in large circles on the grass. He took the bread and the fish in his hands. He looked up toward heaven and gave thanks to God.

Then Jesus broke the bread into pieces. He divided the fish, too. "Give the food to the people," he told his disciples.

The disciples moved toward the crowd. They bent down to hand pieces of bread and fish to the people nearest them. Somehow there was enough for all the people in the first circle.

Then they moved to the next circle . . . and the next . . . and the next. And still there was plenty of food! On and on they went, to the very edges of the crowd.

"We have seen a miracle," they said. "We had five loaves of bread and two fish. Yet there was enough for everybody!"

"God gives more than enough," said Jesus. "Pick up what is left. We must not waste the food God has given us."

So each disciple took a large basket and filled it with the broken pieces of bread and fish that were left over. Twelve big baskets in all!

Jesus sent the people home. Now they were not hungry or sick. They were not lonely or sad. They knew that God was with them.

He sent his disciples away, too. "I will meet you across the lake," he said.

And Jesus went up into the hills by himself to pray.

God Is With You!

From house to house in the city of Capernaum people told the news. "Jesus is back! He is at Peter the fisherman's house!"

Soon Peter's little house was full of people. There was no space left to walk. Even the doorway was filled with people. And when four men came carrying their sick friend on a stretcher bed, they could not get into the house.

The men were disappointed. Their friend was very sick. He could not move at all. They were sure Jesus

could make him well. If only Jesus could see him! But
what could they do? How could they get near Jesus?

Then the men had an idea. They climbed the outside steps to the flat roof. They made a hole in the roof,
just big enough for the bed to get through. Slowly they
lowered their sick friend on his bed mat into the room
below.

How surprised the people inside the house were to see a bed coming through the roof! They crowded back to make room for the sick man and his bed. They reached up to help.

"Be careful!" they said to the men on the roof.

"Can you reach him yet?" called the four friends.

"Almost. . . . Now we have him!"

But the sick man felt afraid. "We should never have come," he thought. "How can Jesus help me?"

At last he felt the hard floor under him. He saw a man bending over him. "Here is Jesus," someone said.

The sick man looked up at Jesus with worried eyes. But Jesus saw how sure the friends were that he could help. So he said to the sick man, "Don't be afraid. God is with you. God loves you."

The worried look went out of the sick man's eyes. "Everything is all right now," he thought. "God loves me. I have never done anything very good. I did not always love God best of all. But God loves me anyway!"

The sick man had never felt so happy.

But in another part of the room there were low, angry voices. "Does Jesus think he is God?"

"It is wrong to talk the way he talks. God will be angry with him!"

Jesus knew what the men were saying. "Why don't you believe me?" he said. "Why don't you believe that I can bring you God's love?"

The men were afraid to answer. "I brought God's love to this man," Jesus said. "That is more important than anything else. It is more important than being able to walk."

Then he said to the man who could not move, "Stand up! Pick up your bed and go home."

Everyone watched to see what would happen. The sick man began to move. He sat up. Jesus reached out and helped him to stand.

"I can walk!" the man said. "Praise God, I can walk!"

Then the man rolled up his bed and tucked it under his arm.

And he ran home to tell his family the wonderful thing that had happened to him.

Inside the house many people were talking at once.

"Surely God has done this!" they said.

"Then it is true! Jesus can bring God near to us. He can bring us God's love."

And they praised God and said, "We never saw anything like this!"

PART

4

A Welcome
for Jesus

HOSANNA! Blessed is he who comes in the
name of the Lord!

MARK 11:9

The Parade

High on a hill in the land where Jesus lived was the great old city of Jerusalem. In all the land, no city was as important as Jerusalem. It was called "the city of God" because the beautiful church called the Temple was there. Once, long before Jesus, a great king named David had lived in Jerusalem. How the people wished that God would send them another king like David!

One day many people were walking to Jerusalem. It was a holiday, and they were going up to Jerusalem to give thanks to God in their beautiful Temple. The people laughed and talked together as they climbed the hill. They sang a song that people in their land had sung for hundreds of years:

"Praise the one who comes to do God's work;
Praise him who comes in the name of the Lord!"

That day, Jesus and his disciples were walking to Jerusalem, too. The people were excited because Jesus was with them. They knew the wonderful things he had done. They liked Jesus.

The people wondered why he was going to Jerusalem. "Maybe he is going to be our king and make our enemies get out of our country!" they guessed.

They believed something wonderful would happen. But the people did not understand what kind of king Jesus really would be. Jesus would be a king of peace and rule over men's hearts. Jesus came to serve people and to help them love God. The people did not understand that kind of king.

On the way to Jerusalem the people came near a little village where Jesus had often visited. Jesus stopped and called two of his disciples.

"Go over to that village," he said. "Just as you come into it, you will find a donkey tied up. Untie it and bring it to me. And if anyone asks why you are untying the donkey, say, 'The Lord needs it; he will send it back right away.'"

The disciples did what Jesus told them. Sure enough, they found a little donkey tied up out in the street. But while they were untying it, some men who were standing there said, "Stop! What are you doing? Why are you untying the donkey?"

The disciples were afraid, but they said what Jesus told them to say, "The Lord needs it; he will send it back right away."

And the men let the disciples take the donkey to Jesus!

Then the disciples took off their coats and put them on the donkey's back. They helped Jesus get up on the donkey.

When the people saw Jesus on the donkey's back, they remembered a song that was written long before they were born:

> Rejoice! Be glad!
> Shout out loud with gladness!
> Look, your king is coming to you,
> Mighty and powerful,
> Lowly, and riding on a donkey.

Now the people were sure that Jesus was going to Jerusalem to be their king!

"Jesus is our king!" someone shouted.

"Hosanna! Praise him who comes in the name of the Lord!" the people sang.

Many pulled off their coats and spread them on the road to make a soft carpet for Jesus to ride on. Others pulled leafy branches from the trees and spread them in his path.

A happy parade marched into the city of Jerusalem. Jesus rode on the little donkey. People shouted and sang for joy. Fathers and mothers waved palm branches in the air. Children gathered flowers from the fields and tossed them along the road. And louder and louder they all sang as they came near the Temple,

"Hosanna! Praise him! Jesus is the king whom God has sent!"

Advent is the name for the days before Christmas. It is a time for getting ready for Jesus. On the first Sunday in Advent, the story of people singing Hosanna to Jesus is read in church. That was how people welcomed Jesus long ago. Even before that, a few people welcomed Jesus when he was a tiny baby. "God will help us," they said. "God loves us." Who were these people?

The Shepherds' Welcome

The winter night was frosty and still. Bright stars twinkled high over the hills near Bethlehem. A cold breeze blew through the olive trees.

Everyone in Bethlehem was asleep. But out on the hills some shepherds were awake. They were guarding their sheep and they huddled close to a low fire. They blew on their hands to warm them. They pulled their warm cloaks tight around their shoulders.

Suddenly the sky was filled with light, light brighter
than day! How frightened the shepherds were!

But an angel of God came to them in the light.
"Do not be afraid," the angel said. "I bring you good
news about a great joy which will come to all the people!

"Today, in the same city where the great king David
was born long ago, a new king has been born. He is the
Lord Jesus, whom God has sent to bring you his love.

He will be your Helper and Friend! Go and see. You will find the baby wrapped in clean cloths and lying in a manger."

And all at once the whole sky was filled with singing angels. "Glory to God in the highest, and peace on earth," they sang.

The shepherds had never heard any song so beautiful. They had never seen anything so wonderful. Even after the angels were gone and only the stars were left to light the sky, they kept on looking up at the place where the angels had been.

"Was it a dream?" they asked one another. But it was no dream. It was really true!

"Let us go to Bethlehem," they said. "Let us go and see this baby the angel told us about."

And so they ran to Bethlehem to find the baby Jesus. They wanted to look in every barn and stable.

They remembered how the angel had said they would find the baby lying in a manger. So they came to the stable in the hillside cave.

And there, inside the stable, they found the carpenter, Joseph, and his wife, Mary. And they found the little Jesus, wrapped in clean cloths, asleep in his manger bed. Everything was just as the angel had told them it would be.

The shepherds told Mary and Joseph what had happened on the hills while they were guarding their sheep. They told about the great light and the angel's glad news.

"We had to come and see," they said. "We had to come and see our little king."

Then the shepherds knelt down beside the manger. They looked at the tiny baby sleeping on the hay. They were sure that God had sent him to bring joy to all the people of the world. And they loved him.

At last the shepherds went back to their sheep. But they could not stop talking about what they had heard and seen.

"Glory to God!" the shepherds said. They said it over and over. "Glory to God! Glory to God!"

Christmas Presents
From Far Away

Far away from the land where Jesus was born lived some men who studied the stars. They liked to watch the stars at night. They knew so much about the names of the stars and planets that they were called wise men.

One night they saw a new star. It was bigger and brighter than any star they had ever seen. "What can it be?" the wise men wondered. "Where did it come from? What can it mean?"

They looked in all their books about the stars, but could not find out about the strange star. The wise men thought and thought. And at last one man remembered something.

"In the land of the Jews, far away," he said, "people have been waiting for God to send them a great king. Maybe this new star means that the great king has been born!"

"We must go and see!" the wise men said. "We must find the king God has sent."

The wise men chose the very best presents they could for the new king. They filled a box with pieces of gold. They took a jar of sweet-smelling incense. They took a precious spice called myrrh. These were the right presents for a king.

And they started out on a journey to the land of the Jews. Week after week their camels' long legs took them swiftly over the desert. At last they came to the land where Jesus lived.

But the wise men did not know where the new king was. They did not even know his name!

"We must go to the most important city," the men decided. "We must ask there for the baby who will be the great king."

And so the wise men came to the big city of Jerusalem. "Where is your little king?" they asked the people. "We have seen his star in the East and have come to worship him."

But nobody knew what the wise men were talking about! "Our king is old," the people said. "His name is Herod. We do not know anything about a new king."

So the wise men went to King Herod's palace. Perhaps they would find the little king there. But King Herod frowned. "I am the king," he said. "There is no other king!"

The wise men told the king about the star. "We are sure God has sent a great new king."

"Could it be true?" Herod asked his wisest men.

"Oh, yes," the men nodded. "It is written in God's book. Someday a great king will be born in Bethlehem."

King Herod felt afraid. "Maybe the king has already been born," he thought. "I don't want anyone else to be king! I want to be king. I must find this child and kill him."

So Herod said to the wise men, "Go to Bethlehem and look for the child. And when you find out where he is, come back and tell me. I want to go and worship him, too."

But Herod was lying. He did not want to worship Jesus at all. He wanted to kill him!

That night, as the wise men rode toward Bethlehem, they saw the bright star again. "There it is!" they shouted. "The star is showing us which way to go!"

In Bethlehem the wise men got down off their camels. They brushed the dust from their long robes. They took out the presents they had carried such a long way.

And when they came into the house, they saw the little Jesus sitting on his mother's lap. Slowly the wise men came near. Their hearts were filled with love for the little boy. They knelt down and bowed their heads.

"Surely God is near!" they said. "Glory to God!"

Then the one wise man opened the box of gold. It shone bright as the sun. "This is for the little king," the man said.

The wise men laid all their presents before Jesus. "We want to give him the best we have," they said.

That same night the wise men had a dream. In the dream God said, "Do not go back to King Herod. He does not love God. He wants to kill the little Jesus."

When morning came, the wise men traveled along another road back to their own country. They were happy because they had found the little Lord Jesus. They had welcomed the king.

PART

5

Jesus Is Always
Our Friend

JESUS said, "I will see you again and your hearts
will rejoice."

JOHN 16:22

People Who Hated Jesus

Jesus loved everybody. He wanted to help everybody love God. He did not care whether people were rich or poor. He did not care whether they were famous or not. He wanted to bring God near to everyone.

But not everybody loved Jesus. Some people did not welcome him the way the shepherds and the wise men did. When Jesus was just a little baby, King Herod wanted to kill him. And when he grew up to be a man, some other men wanted to kill him, too.

These men thought they were very good men. They obeyed all the laws. They went to the Temple every day. "Look at us," they said. "See how good we are."

These men hated Jesus. They did not like the way he healed people who were lame and sick and blind. "It is not right to heal people on the day for prayer," they said. "Jesus does not obey God's laws."

"He eats with people who are bad," they said. "He is kind to people who have done wrong things."

"He says God is his Father!" they said. "He thinks
he is just as important as God!"

One day Jesus went to the beautiful Temple in Jerusalem. He wanted to pray to God. He wanted to help
the people.

But when he got to the Temple, he heard loud voices. He saw men selling pigeons and sheep, right in the Temple courtyard! He saw tables where people were buying coins to use in the Temple. Everywhere people were shoving and pushing and trying to be first to buy.

Jesus was very angry. A church is not a place for buying and selling!

Jesus walked right up to the men who were buying and selling in the Temple. "God's house is a place of prayer," he said. "But you have turned it into a den of robbers!"

Then he pushed over the tables where the men were selling Temple money. Crash! A pile of coins rolled over the floor. He pushed over the tables where other men were selling things. He told the men to get out of the Temple. He drove the animals out, too.

Then the men who had things to sell hated Jesus. They shook their fists at him. They said angry things. The men in charge of the Temple were angry, too.

But many people loved Jesus more than ever. "He did what was right," they said. "He is very brave."

They listened as Jesus told them about God. Blind people and lame people came to the Temple and Jesus healed them. Little children sang, "Hosanna! Hosanna! Hosanna!"

But when the men who hated Jesus heard the singing, they were angry. "Don't you hear what they are singing?" they said to Jesus.

"Yes, I hear them," Jesus said. "But why are you angry? The children are praising God."

The next day Jesus came to the Temple again. He began to teach the people.

The men who hated Jesus wanted to arrest Jesus and kill him. But they were afraid to do that because so many people who loved Jesus were there.

Then Jesus said to the men who hated him, "How sorry I am for you! God wants to come to you, but you will not let him. You obey all the laws, but you are not kind. You do not care about people who are poor or weak or sad. You do not try to help them. You only think about yourselves! You always want to sit in the best seats. You want everyone to think you are so important. You bring gifts to God, but you do not love God!"

There were tears in Jesus' eyes. "I wanted to help you so much," he said. "But you would not let me."

Friends Who Were Afraid

The disciples loved Jesus very much. They were his very best friends. They tried to do what God wanted them to do. They tried to be brave and to love God the way Jesus did.

But even these good friends sometimes made Jesus sad. Sometimes they were selfish. Sometimes they quarreled. Sometimes they were afraid. They did not always obey God.

One night Jesus and his twelve friends were having supper. After supper they sang a song:

The LORD is on my side to help me;

I am not afraid . . .

O give thanks to the LORD, for he is good;

for his steadfast love endures for ever!

It was a brave song. It was a happy song of praise to God!

But Jesus knew that soon his enemies were coming to kill him. "Tonight the soldiers will come," he told

his friends. "They will arrest me and kill me. And you will all run away and leave me."

Then one friend named Peter said, "I won't, Lord! Even if everyone else runs away and leaves you, I will never run away!"

Jesus knew how much Peter loved him. "You are sure now, Peter," he said. "But before the rooster crows

tomorrow morning, you will say that you don't even
know me."

Peter was sure he would never say that! He loved
Jesus and he was proud to be Jesus' friend. "Even if they
kill me, I won't say it", he told Jesus.

And all the other disciples said, "Oh no, Lord!
We won't run away. We will never leave you!"

111

Jesus told his disciples not to worry. "God is with me; I am not alone," he said. "I am going away. But in a little while I will see you again. Now you are sad, but then you will be very happy. Then you will be with me always."

Then Jesus told his disciples something very important to remember.

"My Father loves you, because you have loved me," he said.

And Jesus asked God to take care of everyone who loved him. He asked God to be near them always.

Then Jesus and his friends went to a quiet place where there were many trees. It was called Gethsemane. Jesus felt very sad and troubled. He asked God to help him do what was right, even if it hurt very much.

That night, when it was very dark, the soldiers did come, just as Jesus said. When Peter saw the men, he shouted, "Don't you touch him! Don't you dare take our Lord away!" And he swung his sword so that it cut off the ear of one of the men.

But Jesus said, "Peter! Put your sword away. I must do what God wants." And he touched the man's ear and healed him.

Peter and all the disciples were afraid. And they ran away and left Jesus with the soldiers.

Peter hid in some dark shadows nearby. He wanted to find out what would happen. He followed the men who took Jesus away. But he was careful to stay far behind so that no one would see him.

The men took Jesus to a big house where the man in charge of the Temple lived. Peter stayed outside in the courtyard. He did not know what to do. "I hope nobody finds out who I am," he thought. "Maybe they will want to hurt me, too!"

Peter shivered. It was very cold. Some of the guards and servants were warming themselves at a fire. Peter moved closer to the fire.

The fire felt warm and good. But one of the maids was looking at Peter. "You are a friend of Jesus, aren't you?" she asked.

Peter was frightened. "No," he said. "I don't even know him."

The men around the fire looked at Peter. "I recognize you," one man said. "You are one of his disciples."

But Peter said, "No, you are wrong; I am not."

After that it was quiet for a long time. Then another man said, "I am sure you are one of Jesus' friends."

But Peter said very loud, "I do not know what you mean. I do not know the man."

And just then a rooster crowed. It was morning. And Peter remembered what Jesus had said: "Before the rooster crows, you will say you do not know me."

How sorry Peter felt then! He ran out of the court-yard and cried and cried, as if his heart would break.

Jesus Is Our Friend Forever

It was Friday. On a hill near Jerusalem stood three big crosses. On each cross a man was nailed. This was the way criminals were killed in the land where Jesus lived. Two of the men were robbers. But the man in the center had done nothing wrong at all. The man was Jesus.

The people who hoped that Jesus would be their king were there. They could not understand why he had to die.

The disciples were there, watching and waiting with the people. They could not forget how they had run away and left Jesus. They felt ashamed and sorry.

The men who hated Jesus were there, too. They laughed at Jesus. "He helped others," they said. "Now let him help himself! If God is really your Father, come down from the cross!"

The soldiers made fun of him, too. "If you are king of these people, save yourself!" they shouted.

But what was Jesus saying? The crowd grew quiet. Jesus was talking to God.

"Father, forgive them," he said. "They do not know what they are doing."

"Forgive them! How can he say that?" the disciples wondered. "How can he love us when we have hurt him so much?" But it was true. Jesus was not angry. He still loved them!

Then the sky became very dark. Blackness covered the sun. After a long time Jesus cried out, "Father, take care of me!" And then he died.

Saturday came, and then Sunday. The disciples were together in a house in Jerusalem. They were very

sad. They did not know what to do now that Jesus was dead. And they were afraid. What if the men who killed Jesus tried to kill them, too?

The disciples talked together about Jesus. They remembered how loving and strong and good he was. "Wherever he went, people felt close to God," they said. "But now he is dead."

Suddenly there was a loud knock at the door. The disciples were frightened. Who could it be?

"We are friends," a voice said. "Hurry! Unlock the door. We have seen Jesus!"

They unlocked the door and pulled the two men inside. "What do you mean? Where did you see him? When?"

"Just now!" one of the friends said. "We were walking along the road and a man came and walked with us. We did not know him at first. But he told us how Jesus had to die because of the bad things people did. He said it was the only way we could be close to God. And he said that Jesus was alive again!"

"Yes," the other friend said eagerly. "And when he ate with us, he took the bread in his hands and thanked God for it. He broke it and gave it to us. And then we knew it was Jesus!"

"But where is he?" the disciples wanted to know.

"We don't know," said the men. "All at once he was gone. We didn't even finish our supper. We ran all the way back to tell you about it!"

And then suddenly, Jesus was there. He stood in the room, right in front of his friends. The disciples were surprised and afraid. How could it be? Were they seeing a ghost?

But Jesus said, "I am really here. Look at my hands and my feet. I am real. Touch me and see."

The disciples were glad and yet they could hardly believe it was true. Jesus was dead. Now he was alive again!

"Did you forget?" Jesus said. "I told you I would come again. You don't have to be afraid anymore. God is close to you. And because I am alive, you will live with God forever.

"That is why I came," said Jesus. "God sent me to show you how much he loves you. He sent me to help you love him.

"And now I send you. You must tell all the people in the world that God loves them because of me. Soon I am going back to my Father. But I am with you always. I am your friend forever."